Emerson, Judy.
    Theodore Roosevelt

Pebble™

First Biographies

Theodore Roosevelt

by Judy Emerson

Consulting Editor: Gail Saunders-Smith, Ph.D.
Consultant: John Allen Gable,
Executive Director, Theodore Roosevelt Association
Oyster Bay, Long Island, New York

Capstone
press
Mankato, Minnesota

Pebble Books are published by Capstone Press
151 Good Counsel Drive, P.O. Box 669, Mankato, Minnesota 56002
http://www.capstonepress.com

1 2 3 4 5 6 09 08 07 06 05 04

Library of Congress Cataloging-in-Publication Data
Emerson, Judy.
    Theodore Roosevelt / by Judy Emerson.
        p. cm.—(First biographies)
    Summary: A simple biography of the man who led the Rough Riders in the
Spanish-American War and became president of the United States after the
assassination of President McKinley in 1901.
    Includes bibliographical references and index.
    ISBN 0-7368-2369-7 (hardcover)
    1. Roosevelt, Theodore, 1858–1919—Juvenile literature. 2. Presidents—United
States—Biography—Juvenile literature. [1. Roosevelt, Theodore, 1858–1919.
2. Presidents.] I. Title. II. Series: First biographies (Mankato, Minn.)
E757.E54 2004
973.91'1'092—dc22   2003015708

Note to Parents and Teachers

The First Biographies series supports national history standards for
units on people and culture. This book describes and illustrates the
life of Theodore Roosevelt. The photographs support early readers
in understanding the text. This book also introduces early readers
to subject-specific vocabulary words, which are defined in the
Glossary. Early readers may need assistance to read some words
and to use the Table of Contents, Glossary, Read More, Internet
Sites, and Index/Word List sections of the book.

Table of Contents

Time Line

1858
born

Early Life

Theodore Roosevelt was born in New York City in 1858. Many people called him Teddy. He was a sick child. Theodore exercised to become healthy.

Theodore at age 4

Time Line

1858
born

1880
marries
Alice Lee

6

Theodore graduated from Harvard University in 1880. He married Alice Lee later that year. They had one child. Theodore was later elected to a state office in New York.

Theodore in 1876

Time Line

1858
born

1880
marries
Alice Lee

1884
wife and
mother die

Cowboy and Soldier

Theodore's wife and his mother both died on the same day in 1884. Theodore was very sad. He traveled west. He worked as a cowboy for three years.

Time Line

1858
born

1880
marries
Alice Lee

1884
wife and
mother die

1886
marries
Edith Carow

Theodore came back
to New York. In 1886,
he married Edith Carow.
They had five children.

Time Line

1858	1880	1884	1886
born	marries Alice Lee	wife and mother die	marries Edith Carow

Theodore joined the U.S. Army in 1898. He fought in the Spanish-American War. He led a group of soldiers called the Rough Riders.

◀ Theodore and the Rough Riders

1898
fights
in war

Time Line

1858 born	1880 marries Alice Lee	1884 wife and mother die	1886 marries Edith Carow

President Roosevelt

Theodore was elected governor of New York in 1898. He became vice president in 1901. When President McKinley was killed, Theodore became president.

1898
fights
in war

1901
becomes
president

Time Line

1858
born

1880
marries
Alice Lee

1884
wife and
mother die

1886
marries
Edith Carow

16

As president, Theodore helped small businesses. He helped save wildlife and forests. He worked with Panama to build the Panama Canal.

◀ Theodore visiting workers as they build the Panama Canal

1898
fights
in war

1901
becomes
president

Time Line

1858
born

1880
marries
Alice Lee

1884
wife and
mother die

1886
marries
Edith Carow

18

In 1909 and 1910,
Theodore traveled to Africa
and Europe. In 1912,
he ran for president again.
This time, he lost.

 Theodore (left) traveling in Africa

1898
fights
in war

1901
becomes
president

1909
begins
to travel

Time Line

1858
born

1880
marries
Alice Lee

1884
wife and
mother die

1886
marries
Edith Carow

Remembering Theodore

Theodore Roosevelt died in 1919. He is remembered as a man who loved being president. The teddy bear was named after him.

| 1898 fights in war | 1901 becomes president | 1909 begins to travel | 1919 dies |

Glossary

cowboy—a ranch worker who herds and cares for cattle

elect—to choose someone as a leader by voting

Panama Canal—a narrow area of water that was dug across land in Panama to connect the Atlantic Ocean and Pacific Ocean; Panama is a country in Central America.

president—the elected leader of a country; in the United States, if a president dies, the vice president becomes the president.

Spanish-American War—a short war in 1898 between the United States and Spain

wildlife—wild animals living in their natural environment

Read More

Burke, Rick. *Theodore Roosevelt.* American Lives. Chicago: Heinemann Library, 2003.

Gaines, Ann. *Theodore Roosevelt: Our Twenty-Sixth President.* Our Presidents. Chanhassen, Minn.: Child's World, 2002.

Green, Robert. *Theodore Roosevelt.* Profiles of the Presidents. Minneapolis: Compass Point Books, 2003.

Internet Sites

FactHound offers a safe, fun way to find Internet sites related to this book. All of the sites on FactHound have been researched by our staff.

Here's how:

1. Visit *www.facthound.com*
2. Type in this special code **0736823697** for age-appropriate sites. Or enter a search word related to this book for a more general search.
3. Click on the Fetch It button.

FactHound will fetch the best sites for you!

Index/Word List

Word Count: 208
Early-Intervention Level: 17

Editorial Credits
Mari C. Schuh, editor; Heather Kindseth, cover designer and illustrator; Enoch Peterson, production designer; Scott Thoms, photo researcher

Photo Credits
Corbis, 8, 10, 20; Bettmann, 12, 16, 18
Library of Congress, cover
The Bridgeman Art Library/New-York Historical Society, New York, 1
Theodore Roosevelt Collection, Harvard College Library, 4, 6, 14

24